CONVERSATION STARTERS WITH GOD 2: JUST THE QUESTIONS!

By GLORIA GIERACH

© 2022 by Gloria Gierach
All rights reserved.
ISBN: 979-8-9855353-2-7

Unless otherwise indicated, all Scripture quotations are from the New King James Bible (NKJV). Copyright © 1982 by Thomas Nelson, Inc. Used by permission. All rights reserved. Scripture quotations marked TPT are from The Passion Translation®. Copyright © 2017, 2018, 2020 by Passion & Fire Ministries, Inc. Used by permission. All rights reserved. ThePassionTranslation.com.

Cover design by Kyle Re Creative

DEDICATION

To *my Beloved Jesus,*

*"May Your awakening breath blow
upon my life until I am fully Yours.
Breathe upon me with Your Spirit wind.
Stir up the sweet spice of Your life within me.
Spare nothing as you make me Your fruitful garden.
Hold nothing back until I release Your fragrance.
Come walk with me as You walked with
Adam in Your paradise garden.
Come taste the fruits of Your life in me."*

Song of Songs 4:16 (TPT)

CONTENTS

ACKNOWLEDGMENTS	1
INTRODUCTION	5
GOD DISCOVERY	22
WHOLENESS DISCOVERY	52
SELF DISCOVERY	84
APPENDIX	116

ACKNOWLEDGMENTS

I am so grateful for my Lord and Savior, Jesus. You brought me into Your heart when I was a young teenager. You wooed me into a deeper and deeper love relationship with You throughout my life. Jesus, You have been my constant companion to Whom I can share everything. Jesus, You are my Beloved!

Thank You, Papa God, for pouring out such love and acceptance on me. You have given me identity as Your beloved child that allows me to walk in confidence of who I am.
You are my Protector and Provider.
You are my Papa God!

Holy Spirit, You have been drawing me and teaching me even before I knew who You were. You have challenged me to step out of my comfort zone and do things I never thought I could. I love Your gentle stirrings in my heart that lead me into encounters with God. Thank You, Holy Spirit, for not leaving me alone, but continuing to pursue me with Your love.

Thank you to my husband, Rich, for always supporting me and encouraging me to pursue my dreams. I would not be who I am if you were not walking through life with me. You are my love and I love doing life with you.
Let's go for another 40 years.

To each of my children –
Joshua, Luke, Isaiah, Hannah,
Paul, Grace and Noelle.

You are a treasure and joy to my life. I am so blessed to have you as my "children". All of you are carrying such huge destinies within you that I am seeing fulfilled before my eyes. I pray that you encounter the Lord in new ways and stand on our shoulders to go so much further in life.

To Kyle Re, for encouraging me and providing suggestions along with the cover for this book. You have partnered with me and Holy Spirit to do some amazing things. Your creativity is always amazing! Thank you!

To James Kinsey for being my God solution to Adobe InDesign. He has been a great friend and lifesaver.

IMPORTANT INFORMATION FOR THE READER

Thank you for purchasing Conversation Starters with God 2. You may have noticed that there is another Conversation Starters with God that is a journal. This book has the same content but without the journaling space. Why did we do this?

1. I found that many people have their own favorite journals and didn't want another journal to write in.
2. You can journal more than one page if you get on a role with God.
3. You can now pick and choose what questions you want to ask God and write His answers in your own journal.
4. There is a spot after each question number for you to write the date that you and God worked through that question. By writing in the date, you can then look back in whatever journal you were writing in at the time to see what God was speaking to you regarding that question.
5. This is a smaller book to carry with you when you spend your time with God.
6. Smaller book means lower price.
7. Conversation Starters with God 2 will be available soon in Ebook format.

I hope that you enjoy your time talking with God using these Conversation Starters with God 2.

Gloria Gierach

INTRODUCTION TO CONVERSATION STARTERS WITH GOD 2: JUST THE QUESTIONS!

INTRODUCTION

I encountered Jesus when I was 14 years old and my life was changed from that day on. I was blessed by God to stay on a path with Him throughout my life. I remember spending time outside where I grew up just talking to God. Did I hear an audible voice? No. But I heard and felt Him in my spirit. I didn't understand it all then but do we ever really understand life with Christ fully? Fast forward to decades later and I am at a meeting with my husband. We are listening to a man talk about his relationship with God and how they talk. I thought, "That sounds like me". After the meeting, my husband says, "That's not how I hear God." (Shock!!!!) Say what? I thought that God spoke to everyone the same way he speaks to me, however I found that He speaks to my husband differently. This revelation was earth shaking and launched me on a journey to understand how God speaks to His people. I started to study Scripture and read books about this topic and discovered some things that I took for granted. I thought everyone experienced God like I did. Not!

I have 7 children (plus spouses and grandchildren) and I interact with each of them differently. I talk about different things with each. It is not that any one of these methods of communication are bad but they are different because our relationship is different. In the same way, God will interact with you differently than He does with me. He will use your love language, your style of speaking, your sense of humor, etc. The Creator of our hearts interacts with us in ways that we can receive and feel His love for us. Isn't that amazing? We cannot comprehend God's immensity and capacity to love each of us individually and pursue us all at the same time. That's the key, though, time. God is not confined by time, but we are. God can be everywhere at once and interacting with everyone all the time. Wow! What a big God we have. I <u>know</u> that God loves to communicate with us His heart of love. I also believe that everyone God loves can hear Him and that includes YOU!

What if you have not heard/sensed God before? Sometimes, we don't recognize His voice/presence because we think it needs to sound and feel a certain way -- maybe expecting the voice of Morgan Freeman or James Earl Jones to come out of the sky. LOL Maybe a few lightning bolts or thunder. If that happens, I think the Fear of the Lord would be all over me. I would much rather hear that still, small voice of the Lord. (1 Kings 19:12) It feels less intimidating and more gentle and loving.

How do we know that God wants to communicate with us? His Word tells us.

- o *John 15:15 "No longer do I call you servants, for a servant does not know what his master is doing; but <u>I have called you friends, for all things that I heard from my Father I have made known to you.</u>"*
- o *John 10:27 "<u>My sheep hear My voice, and I know them and they follow Me.</u>"*
- o *Jeremiah 33:3 "<u>Call to me and I will answer you, and show you great and mighty things, which you do not know.</u>"*

These are just a few of the verses in the Bible. There are many illustrations of God speaking to His people throughout the Bible.

I have heard the comparison of God speaking to you as being like a butterfly that lands on your shoulder. If you move slowly and turn your head toward the butterfly, you can enjoy its beauty and presence. It is the same with God's voice. You must turn your heart toward God's voice then you can hear the spontaneous thoughts He has for you. The more we draw closer to God the more we will hear what He has to say to us. It is a relationship. The closer the relationship, the more we hear God's heart for us and others. It is just like our relationships on earth. We can keep it "relationship lite – great taste but less filling" or we can choose the road to intimacy with the Creator of the Universe. God wants to reveal His nature to you and rewire your brain with Kingdom thinking and living.

There are two resources (of many) that I recommend that will help you to hear God better if you are new to this whole arena.
- Shawn Bolz "Translating God: Hearing God's Voice for Yourself and the World Around You."
- Mark and Patti Virkler workbook "How to hear God's Voice".

In Virkler's book, they speak of 4 keys to hearing God's voice.
1. Recognize God's voice as spontaneous thoughts which light upon your mind.
2. Quiet yourself so you can hear God's voice.

3. Look for vision as you pray. Allowing God to communicate with us via the eyes of our hearts/understanding. (Ephesians 1:18)
4. Write down the flow of thoughts and pictures that come to you by journaling. Journaling is recording your thoughts/questions/prayers and listening for what you sense to be God's responses -- a dialogue with God.

That is what this book is all about. Recording your conversations with God regarding numerous topics in order to know and experience God and His love for you.

Along this journey, I learned that God speaks in many ways that, sometimes, we don't always pick up on. Here is a list of <u>some of the ways</u> that God speaks.

1. **Dreams** - Dreams can be categorized as self-condition, healing, calling, chemical, courage, correction, direction, intercession, revelation, warfare, deliverance, soulish, warning, encouragement, etc.
People in Scripture who had dreams –
Joseph, Daniel, Joseph (father of Jesus), Nebuchadnezzar, Magi, Baker, Cupbearer, Laban, Abimelech, Jacob, Solomon. *(Job 33:14-18; Numbers 12:6; Genesis 40:8)*
(Suggestion: Keep paper and pen by your bed at night so that if God gives you a dream you can write it down immediately.)
For information about how to interpret dreams, check out Streams Ministries, Doug Addison, and Barbie Breathitt for resources.

2. **Colors** - Colors can have a positive meaning or a negative meaning. Red = passion, Jesus' blood OR anger, lust *(See Color Meanings in the Appendix)*
3. **Visions** - Pictures/movies seen while awake with eyes open or closed. *(Daniel Ch. 8 & 10; Acts 10:3-6; 10:9-16; 16:9; Isaiah 6)*
4. **Trances** - Dream-like state when we are awake. *(Acts 10:9-11; 11:4-5)*
5. **Taste** - *(Psalms 34:8; 119:103; Proverbs 24:13-14)* We have 5 senses in the physical and in the spiritual (sight, hearing, touch, smell and taste). We are to "train our senses to distinguish good and evil." *(Hebrews 5:14)*
6. **Hearing** - An audible voice or inner voice that you hear with your spirit. *(1 Samuel 3:10; 1 Kings 19:12)*
7. **Touch/Feel** - By physical contact with someone or something, a person may sense someone's physical feelings or emotions. God can also touch you with His Spirit. *(Mark 5:27; Matthew 19:13)*
8. **Smell** - Associated with temple worship, perfume with which Mary anointed Jesus' feet, fragrance is attributed to the knowledge of Christ, those who follow and proclaim Christ, the sacrifice of Christ, the gifts of believers to a missionary, acceptable sacrifices and pious conduct are called a "sweet smell" or "savor" well-pleasing to God *(Exo. 29:18; 2 Chron. 2:4; 13:11; John 11:2; 12:3-5; 2 Cor. 2:14-16; Eph. 5:2; Phil. 4:18)*
9. **Bible** - The Holy Spirit uses the Bible to speak to us. *(Psalms 119:105; Heb. 4:12)* Everything we get from God should be in agreement with Scripture.

10. **Impressions** - God seems to direct/impress upon you to interact with the world around you. *(Mark 2:8-12; 5:25-34; Acts 16:6)*
11. **Creation** - God can use all His creation to give us messages from Him. *(Psalms 19:1-4; Luke 3:21-22)*
12. **Circumstances** – open or closed doors, divine appointments and connections. *(Psalms 37:23; Proverbs 3:6; Acts 19:8-9; 1 Cor. 16:9)*
13. **Numbers** - have meaning in Scripture. *Something repeated more than one time increases the power of the statement. Be hesitant to use numbers for direction of any kind. If they are direction, God will confirm it elsewhere. (See number meanings in the Appendix)*
14. **Angels** - God still sends angels - protection, messenger, ministering, judgment, worshiping, healing, etc. *(Psa. 91:11; 1 Kings 19; 2 Kings 19:35; Matt. 4:11; Luke 1; John 5; Acts 8:26)*
15. **Songs** - God uses the lyrics of a song to touch us dramatically. God sings songs in the night over us. *(Job 35:10; Zeph. 3:17)*
16. **Word of Knowledge** - To know something you didn't know before or know normally. Word of Knowledge can also be used to know what God wants to heal in someone else through an ache or pain in your body that wasn't there before. *(2 Samuel 12:1-14; John 1:48; 4:17-18; Acts 27:21-26)*
17. **Word of Wisdom** - Supernatural revelation of wise advice, direction, or knowledge for future action. It is often demonstrated in applying scriptures, insight, guidance, or counsel. *(James 3:17)*

18. Memories, Flashbacks, Visitations, Divine Translation/Transportation, Movies, billboards, license plates, books, magazines, etc., - Any way that God wants to speak!!

God can speak to us any way He wants and that we need. So how do we know if it is God? Good question. Not everything we sense/hear is from God. Not every thought that you have is your thoughts. So how do you discern? From my research, there are at least 4 voices that we can listen to. Sometimes, they overlap with our own voice. What are these voices?

1. Our Own Voice
This voice is mixed with our belief systems and our personal feelings. It includes our personal preferences and desires. There are times that we want something so badly that we convince ourselves (and those around us) that this is what God wants too. If what we are hearing or sensing primarily caters to our own comforts and desires, we should ask God for unbiased confirmations. Our own voice is also our analytical thoughts and our reasoning process. That analytical and reasoning process can argue away everything God is speaking to you.

2. Other People's Voices
These voices are not to be confused with those people who give us godly counsel. Other people's voices refer to what we have been taught or experienced through life. It is our histories with people that mold us, sometimes detrimentally. They create a filter through which we see life. What we have been told about ourselves and our world (even at an early age) will become those things we believe about ourselves. If these are in disagreement with God's

truth, they are lies and distort our ability to hear from God clearly.

3. The Enemy/Satan's Voice

The Enemy/Satan masquerades as an angel of light. What you hear or sense from these voices will line up with the names/character of Satan, which include Accuser, Adversary, Liar, Destroyer, Thief and Murderer, etc. Often it feels like our own thoughts but are thoughts the enemy placed into our minds that are contrary to God's Word. i.e., offensive thoughts during worship. Satan will bring condemnation, guilt and shame. Satan wants you to question God's character and turn you away from Him. *("God doesn't answer my prayers. He only answers other people's prayers".)* The enemy brings incessant accusations that God is not talking to you at all and that you can't hear God! Satan will also use well-meaning people to speak words that could water down your faith. *("God doesn't want to heal everybody. He gives some people illness to build their character or increase their faith".)* Satan will often quote Scripture and use spiritual-sounding language. *(Luke 4:1-12)* Satan's goal is to confuse, entrap and derail. It is important to know the Word so that you can identify the lies.

4. God's Voice

God's voice will line up with the names/character of God -- Edifier, Comforter, Teacher, Creator, Healer, Giver of Life, Protector, Deliverer, Provider, Lover, Kind, Good, etc. It is expressed through our personality and style of speech. It does not bypass or eradicate our personality or style of speech. God is united with you (I Cor. 6:17) and flowing out through you. God's voice is often spontaneous thoughts which light upon your mind. They are often light and gentle, and easily cut off by any exertion of self (your own thoughts, will, etc.), They will have an unusual content to them, in that they will be wiser, more healing, more loving and more motive-oriented than your thoughts. When God speaks to you, it causes a special reaction within you, such as a sense of excitement, conviction, faith, life, awe, or peace. Even when God convicts you of sin, it is filled with His love and hope. All we need to do is repent to experience His pleasure again. *(1 John 1:9)*

Whose voice are you listening to?

Whenever thoughts are hostile to the Word of God or distort the Word, we are told to demolish them *(2 Corinthians 10:4-6)*. You are to silence the devil with the Word *(Matthew 4:1-11)*, resist the devil and he will flee from you *(James 4:7)*.

Satan doesn't want you to hear God's voice because you will be quickly transformed by it. The enemy is scared to death about your potential transformation, because the more you are transformed, the more you will become a Christian who changes all those you come into contact with.

A few other things to mention here:

Assumptions, opinions, and doctrines can affect our ability to accurately interpret what we are sensing. Don't force your revelation into your grid of understanding.

God usually speaks to us through symbolic <u>spiritual metaphors</u>. A metaphor figuratively explains something by making a comparison with the similarities of something that is technically unrelated. Examples:

- falling = losing control, anxious, backsliding
- house = you, your life, your family, body of Christ
- naked = vulnerable, transparent, purity, exposed

<u>You must rely on the Holy Spirit to interpret what you are hearing/sensing.</u>

Don't evaluate too much, just engage. If you take more than a few seconds to evaluate your impressions, then you are probably being too logical. When you are logical, you tend to reason it out of your way. Just start journaling what you see or feel without analyzing it and trust that God will give you more as you go.

I've put some basic questions together for you on the next page to evaluate what you are hearing in order to discern if it is from God or not.

Six Filters/Questions for What You Are Receiving

1. **Does it agree with Scripture?** Everything you hear must be in accord with the heart of the Word (the Bible). Some things are not found in the literal Word but are not wrong. For example, you will not find a Scripture that says, "Take the job at the manufacturing plant." You will find Scriptures that will impress on you a direction. Let God show you. *(2 Timothy 3:16-17; Ps. 12:6)*

2. **Does it glorify God and direct you and others to Jesus?** *(John 15:26-27; John 16:14; 1 Cor. 6:19-20; Deut. 13:1-5)*

3. **What kind of fruit does it produce?** True revelation produces fruit in character and conduct that agrees with the fruit of the Holy Spirit. It releases the Spirit of Adoption with liberty and not bondage. It produces life and not death. If it is God's voice, even if it is unclear at first, the revelation will release peace and be confirmed in your spirit. *(Rom. 8:15; 1 Cor. 14:33; 2 Cor. 3:6; Gal. 5:22-23; Col. 3:15-16; 2 Tim. 1:7)*

4. **Where are your eyes and heart postured?** The anointing of the Holy Spirit guides us toward the Truth. If you posture your heart properly, the flow within is likely to be the Holy Spirit! You must place yourself in a listening posture to hear God's voice. *Test your thoughts by knowing where your eyes are fixed.* The flow comes out of the vision you hold before your eyes. *(1 John 2:20, 26-27)*

5. **Is it consistent with the ways and nature of God?** Is the word/picture more in character with God's nature of loving, comforting, affirming, protecting, imparting identity, etc.? Or is the word more consistent with Satan's character of lies/lying, accusing, condemning, destroying, etc.? *(Ps 103:2-5, 8; Matt 7:15-20; Gal 5:22-23)*

6. **If it is in regards to the future, does it come true?** *(Deut. 18:20-22)* If a revelation contains a prediction concerning the future, are these predictions fulfilled? If not, with a few exceptions, the revelation is not from God. Examples of exceptions:
    - Your timing is off.
    - The will of the people involved.
    - National repentance – example of Ninevah
    - Messianic Predictions – hundreds of years until fulfilled

Are you ready to start your adventure with God?

The intention of this book is to spark interaction between you and God. These discussions with God will warm your heart, stimulate your mind and inspire life lessons. God will inspire you to discover, examine, understand, heal and be empowered to walk in your destiny. The questions are designed to break down communication barriers and cultivate connection, openness, transparency and vulnerability with your God. By journaling, you are able to easily recall what God is speaking to you and evaluate what "voice" you are listening to. Before you know it, you will have an amazing dialogue with God.

There are 3 sections to this book. You can jump around or go through it page by page. Each section carries a different part of your journey with God. They are:

1. **God Discovery** – Who is God and how do I interact with Him and He with me?

2. **Wholeness Discovery** – Questions to work through relationship and personal issues and hindrances that could be holding you back and crippling you.

3. **Self Discovery** – Who am I and what is my destiny/calling?

Below are questions to ask God that will help you to more fully understand what you are sensing from Him.

Questions of God to Understand What You Are Hearing/Sensing

1. Why are You showing me this?
2. What are You trying to tell me through this?
3. How will this help me?
4. Are there any scriptures you want to highlight to me concerning this?
5. How can I apply what you are showing me?
6. What else do I need to know about this?
7. How can I partner with You concerning this word?

Prayer:

*Father, I come in the name of the Lord, Jesus Christ. I am asking for a special gift of grace to be deposited right now inside of me to enter into this adventure with You. Let a gift of grace come to me that would enable me, with confidence, to hear Your voice. Increase my capacity and appetite for hearing. Lord, I ask for You to release the gift of revelation over me so that I can hear clearly what you want to say to me and to those around me. Fill me with Your Holy Spirit. Wrap around me with Your love, peace and presence. Guide me into Your truth and freedom.
Thank You! In Jesus' name. Amen.*

GOD DISCOVERY

WHO IS GOD?
HOW DO I INTERACT WITH HIM?
HOW DOES HE INTERACT WITH ME?

*Jesus replied, "Loving Me empowers you to obey
My Word. And My Father will love you so deeply that
We will come to you and make you
Our dwelling place.
(John 14:23 - TPT)*

Q1
Surprise me by telling me something about You!

_____
Date Answered

Q2
What are Your thoughts about healing for today?

_____
Date Answered

Q3
There is mention in Scripture of other creatures in Heaven. Can You tell me about some of them?

_____
Date Answered

Q4
Father God, how are You different from Jesus Christ and Holy Spirit?

_____
Date Answered

Q5
God, what do You consider to be supernatural?

_____
Date Answered

Q6

God, I love You! What would You like to speak to me about today?

_____
Date Answered

Q7

What is Your favorite way to communicate with me? Is it different for each of the Trinity?

_____
Date Answered

Q8

Teach me how to recognize Your presence and anointing. What does it feel like when You are here? What does it feel like when You lift Your presence from me?

_____
Date Answered

Q9

What is an aspect of Your character/nature that I don't know yet?

_____
Date Answered

Q10

If someone has never heard of You, God,
what would you want me to tell them about You?

Date Answered

Q11

Jesus, what did You mean when You said,
*"I am the Way, the Truth, and the Life. No one
comes to the Father except through Me"?
(John 14:6)*

Date Answered

Q12

Father God, how have You been my Provider
throughout my life?

Date Answered

Q13

God, what brings You joy?
What makes You laugh out loud?

Date Answered

Q14

Why do You let good things happen to bad people?
Why do You let bad things happen to good people?

_____
Date Answered

Q15

Jesus, how have You shown Yourself as
my Companion and Friend?

_____
Date Answered

Q16

Jesus, the Bible says You are praying for me.
(*Hebrews 7:25*)
What are You praying for me at this time?

_____
Date Answered

Q17

What aspect of You, God, do I need to
draw upon at this time in my life?

_____
Date Answered

Q18

Holy Spirit, how have You been my Comforter throughout my life?

_____
Date Answered

Q19

Are there sports in Heaven?
How are they different from here?

_____
Date Answered

Q20

Tell me how You are aware of me today, Jesus.
What in my life has Your attention?

_____
Date Answered

Q21

Would You show me and help me experience Your wrap-around presence right now?
How do I partner with Holy Spirit to experience and encounter You?

_____
Date Answered

Q22

God, how can I love You well today?

_____
Date Answered

Q23

Have You ever sent angels to protect me or
to tell me something? Tell me about that time.

_____
Date Answered

Q24

Do I have a guardian angel?
Can You tell me his name?
Have I kept him busy over the years?

_____
Date Answered

Q25

Jesus, how are You different from
Father God and Holy Spirit?

_____
Date Answered

Q26

Why don't I see miracles and healings much today?

_____
Date Answered

Q27

Jesus, how have You communicated with me?
Are there times I haven't recognized it as You?

_____
Date Answered

Q28

Holy Spirit, how have You nurtured me
throughout my life?

_____
Date Answered

Q29

Jesus, what did You love about being
on earth as a man?

_____
Date Answered

Q30

Jesus, was there a miracle You did while on earth
that brought you great joy? Why?

_____
Date Answered

Q31

Holy Spirit, why did You show Yourself
as tongues of fire at Pentecost? *(Acts 2:1-4)*

_____
Date Answered

Q32

What does the Bible mean when it says to "store up
treasures in Heaven"? *(Matthew 6:19-21)*

_____
Date Answered

Q33

What does walking in the Fear of the Lord look like?
(Psalm 25:12, 34:9, 111:10; Isaiah 11:2-3)

_____
Date Answered

Q34

Father God, Jesus, and Holy Spirit, what are Your love languages?
(Words of Affirmation, Touch, Acts of Service, Gifts, Quality Time or ???)

_____
Date Answered

Q35

Is there a question You want to ask me? What is it? What question have You been waiting for me to ask You?

_____
Date Answered

Q36

What is Heaven like?
Tell me one or more things about it.

_____
Date Answered

Q37

Father God, how have You been my Protector throughout my life?

_____
Date Answered

Q38

Will I recognize people who already died when I go to Heaven?

_____
Date Answered

Q39

Is there a book of the Bible I should study? Why?

_____
Date Answered

Q40

Is there a Bible character I should study? Why?

_____
Date Answered

Q41

God, what did You feel/think when man disobeyed You in the garden?

_____
Date Answered

Q42

Father God, what did You feel/think when You watched Your Son, Jesus, dying on the cross?

_____
Date Answered

Q43

Jesus, what were You thinking/feeling when You were made fun of, beaten and whipped?

_____
Date Answered

Q44

Jesus, what were You thinking/feeling when You were on the cross?

_____
Date Answered

Q45

Is there something I believe about You, God, that is not consistent with Your Word? What is the truth?

_____
Date Answered

Q46

Holy Spirit, how have You been my Teacher in life?

_____
Date Answered

Q47

Read *John 7:38-39*. Lord, how important is this "river"? What happens if I neglect the river and live out of my own initiative? What else do I need to know about the river in me?

_____
Date Answered

Q48

Enter a Bible story by picturing the scene with you in it. Ask God what He wants You to see or understand. (Examples: *Matthew 8:5-13; 14:22-33; Mark 5:21-34; Luke 17:11-19; John 6:1-14*)

_____
Date Answered

Q49

Holy Spirit, how are You different from Father God and Jesus?

_____
Date Answered

Q50

I want to learn to hear You more accurately, so I want to practice. What topic will the Pastor speak on next Sunday? Who will call me today? What songs will be sung on Sunday? Look back next week to check your accuracy.

_____
Date Answered

Q51

Lord, what is on Your mind today?
What are You thinking about?

_____
Date Answered

Q52

Jesus, if You walked the earth today, would I be
one of Your disciples? Why or why not?

_____
Date Answered

Q53

What does my mansion in Heaven look like?
What is one feature that I will love?

_____
Date Answered

Q54

Jesus, how have You been active in my life
in the last 24 hours?

_____
Date Answered

Q55

Jesus, what is something You love about Father
God that You want to remind me of today?

_____
Date Answered

Q56

Father God, how do You feel when I come knocking at Your door?

_____
Date Answered

Q57

What animal noise do You enjoy the most? Why? What animal noise makes You laugh?

_____
Date Answered

Q58

Jesus, how have You been pursuing me this week?

_____
Date Answered

Q59

Jesus, where are You in the room and what are You doing?

_____
Date Answered

Q60

What would You like me to read in the Bible today? Why do You want me to read it?

_____
Date Answered

Q61

Tell him how much you appreciate Him and how special He is to you. Then, let Jesus speak back to you of His love for you.

_____
Date Answered

Q62

Jesus, how did You do it? How did You maintain such an easy, intimate connection with Father God here on earth?

_____
Date Answered

Q63

You say that I am the fragrance/aroma of Christ. What does that smell like? (*2 Corinthians 2:15*)

_____
Date Answered

Q64

What is Your favorite movie? Why?

_____
Date Answered

Q65

Read *Matthew 16:13-19*.
Jesus, how did it impact You when Peter called out Your true identity as the "Son of the Living God"?

_____
Date Answered

Q66

Is there a new way that You would like to speak to me that You haven't before?

_____
Date Answered

Q67

Father, how do You pay attention to all of us at the same time? I have a hard time staying focused on even one thing!

_____
Date Answered

Q68

Lord, what is one thing You would like to change about the world?
How can I partner with You in it?

_____
Date Answered

Q69

How do You feel about tithing today?
What does it look like for me?
(Numbers 18:26; Proverbs 3:9-10; Malachi 3:10)

_____
Date Answered

Q70

What song are You singing over me right now
in this season? *(Zephaniah 3:17)*

_____
Date Answered

Q71

When You called James and John, they left their
business and Dad behind to run down the beach
after You. *(Luke 5:1-11)* What was going on in Your
heart in that moment?

_____
Date Answered

Q72

Is there anyone else out there in the universe
besides us on the earth?

_____
Date Answered

Q73

What is one thing I'm doing/believing now that makes You proud? Why?

_____
Date Answered

Q74

What is something You care deeply about that I don't fully understand yet? How can I grow in that?

_____
Date Answered

Q75

God, You are a good God. Where have I been partnering with negative life expectations and not expected Your goodness?
How can I change that?

_____
Date Answered

Q76

Jesus, what are the rewards that I have yet to see or experience? (Matthew 6:3-4,6,18; Luke 6:35; Colossians 3:23-24)

_____
Date Answered

Q77

How do I view You, Father God, and what do I think about when I think about You? How do You, Father God, see me, and what do You say about me? Father God, is there anything I need to deal with so that I can have a right picture of who You are?

_____
Date Answered

Q78

How do I view You, Jesus, and what do I think about when I think about You? How do You, Jesus, see me, and what do You say about me? Jesus, is there anything I need to deal with so that I can have a right picture of who You are?

_____
Date Answered

Q79

How do I view You, Holy Spirit, and what do I think about when I think about You? How do You, Holy Spirit, see me, and what do You say about me? Holy Spirit, is there anything I need to deal with so that I can have a right picture of who You are?

_____
Date Answered

Q80

What does it look and feel like to be hidden with Christ in God? *(Colossians 3:3)*

_____
Date Answered

Q81

God, would You teach me about You as my quiet retreat, wrap-around presence, and my shield with Your Word?
"You're my place of quiet retreat, and Your wrap-around presence becomes my shield as I wrap myself in Your Word." (Psalm 119:114 - TPT)

_____
Date Answered

Q82

What is fear? How is fear and Fear of the Lord different? What do I need to understand so that ungodly fear has no place in my life?

_____
Date Answered

Q83

How am I connected to the vine? (*John 15:1-8*)

_____
Date Answered

Q84

You say that I can do all things through Christ, who strengthens me. What are the "all things"?
(*Philippians 4:13*)

_____
Date Answered

Q85

Father God, how are You intimate and involved in my life?

_____
Date Answered

Q86

Write your questions for the Lord and then write His answers. Keep writing until God is done with the dialogue.

_____
Date Answered

Q87

If we were to take a road trip together, where would You want to go and why?

_____
Date Answered

Q88

Lord, are You excited to be with me? Why?

_____
Date Answered

Q90

How is Your love different from the love
I experience in the world?

_____
Date Answered

Q91

Why did You make clouds to look so different?
Do You like to show people things/shapes in Your
clouds? How should I view storms in the physical
and in life?

_____
Date Answered

Q92

What are some spiritual blessings that You have for
me that I need to walk in? (*Ephesians 1:3*)

_____
Date Answered

Q93

Do You care about my feelings?
Why did you create feelings?

_____
Date Answered

Q94

Jesus, what is on today's menu? How do You
want to satisfy my desire for Your goodness today?
(*Psalm 107:9*)

Date Answered

Q95

How has Your goodness and mercy been following
me in the last week? (*Psalm 23:6*)

Date Answered

Q96

Let's celebrate our relationship!
What do You want to do together today?
Do You have an adventure You want us to go on?

Date Answered

Q97

Do You ever get tired of making sunrises and
sunsets? What do You love about them?

Date Answered

Q98
Holy Spirit, let's remember the times You have shifted my circumstances in answer to my cry. Take me back to one of those memories so we can rejoice in it together!

_____
Date Answered

Q99
Why did You consider David a "Man after Your Heart"? *(1 Samuel 13:14)*

_____
Date Answered

Q100
God, You speak all the love languages. Is there a love language I enjoy having You speak to me more than others? (Words of Affirmation, Touch, Acts of Service, Gifts, Quality Time or ???)

_____
Date Answered

Q101
Father God, how do You sing and celebrate over me? *(Zephaniah 3:17)*

_____
Date Answered

Q102

Is it important to memorize Bible verses? Why? What verses do You want me to memorize?

Date Answered

Q103

It is hard to believe that You, God, love me completely and unconditionally. Is there anything hiding in my heart that says I have to change, be better, or do something different to earn Your love? How do I change my thinking about Your love for me?

Date Answered

Q104

What does it mean to have childlike faith?
(Matthew 18:3; Mark 10:14; Luke 18:17)

Date Answered

Q105

Father God, how do I wait for the Lord?
(Psalm 27:14, 33:20, 37:7&34, 130:5)

Date Answered

Q106
Why did You create time?

_____
Date Answered

Q107
Lord, how am I Your lover?
How do You watch over me like a bodyguard?
"God, you watch carefully over all Your lovers like a bodyguard." (Psalm 145:20 - TPT)

_____
Date Answered

Q108
What treasure do I have that I can
bring to you today?

_____
Date Answered

Q109
Jesus, who could we surprise by telling them
who they really are in Your eyes today?

_____
Date Answered

Q110
How do You want to be present in
my conversations today?

_____
Date Answered

Q111

What is one way that I can be less "grown-uppity" and more like a child with You today that You would really enjoy?

Date Answered

Q112

Jesus, what did I do today that made You laugh?

Date Answered

Q113

Jesus, is there a special place in the spirit that You want to take me to in order to help me encounter You there? What does it look like to relax with You?

Date Answered

Q114

Father God, who is a hero in Your eyes? What makes them a hero?

Date Answered

Q115

Is there fun and laughter in Heaven? What do people enjoy doing there?

Date Answered

Q116

Holy Spirit, would You show me a picture of how You see me right now?

_____
Date Answered

Q117

Where is the most beautiful place on earth? Why do You think it is the most beautiful?

_____
Date Answered

Q118

How do I know that You are real, God?

_____
Date Answered

Q119

If You do something "out of the box" or new, how do I know it is You since I've never seen or heard of You doing this before?

_____
Date Answered

Q120

You want us to dance in praise and worship before You. Why do You enjoy that and how can I please You with dancing before You when I don't dance well? *(Psalm 149:3; 150:4)*

_____
Date Answered

Q121

There are animals and sea creatures that have never been seen by man. Why did You create them? Is all of Your creation for man to enjoy or did You make some that You are the only one who sees and enjoys them?

_____
Date Answered

Q122

Why did You create black holes and what is in a black hole?

_____
Date Answered

Q123

Do I have a "secret place" with You? Can You take me there now so that I can enjoy Your presence and communion? Is there anything I should bring with me to this secret place with You?
(Psalm 31:20; 91:1; Matthew 6:6, 18)

_____
Date Answered

Q124

What is the weather like in Heaven?
What will the weather be like on the "new earth"?
Will everyone like the weather?
(Revelations 21:1)

Date Answered

Q125

What did You think about when You were designing the days of my life before any of them were even existent?
(Psalm 139:16)

Date Answered

WHOLENESS DISCOVERY

SEEKING PERSONAL WHOLENESS BY WORKING WITH GOD THROUGH RELATIONSHIP STRUGGLES, PERSONAL ISSUES AND HINDRANCES.

"...When you continue to embrace all that I teach, you prove that you are my true followers. For if you embrace the truth, it will release true freedom into your lives."
(John 8:31-32 - TPT)

Q126

If I didn't have You, Lord, what would my life have looked like? How would my lack of relationship with You impact other people?

_____
Date Answered

Q127

What does healthy boundaries look like in my life? Is there an area of my life that I need healthier boundaries?

_____
Date Answered

Q128

Is there an area of my life that I have abdicated (given up) my authority and responsibility?

_____
Date Answered

Q129

What limiting belief (or lie) holds me back the most in life? If I give You this lie, what would You like to give me in exchange that will shift my paradigm of thinking?

_____
Date Answered

Q130
What does freedom for me look like to You?

_____
Date Answered

Q131
Think about the most painful thing you've gone through in your life. God, how did You meet me during that painful time?

_____
Date Answered

Q132
Is there an area of my life that I am expecting something negative instead of Your goodness? (Possible life areas: Finances, Relationships, Job/Occupation, Health, Church, Prayer)

_____
Date Answered

Q133
What we do with our days will eventually become how we're known and remembered. Jesus, when You look at my life on an average day, what would You say about my impact and faith?

_____
Date Answered

Q134

How can I love my family better?
How can I show my family who You are?

Date Answered

Q135

<u>Parents:</u> Lord, tell me how You see each of my children. Are there any special instructions? What are the gifts and talents You have given them that You want me to focus on in order to help nurture and develop them?
<u>Non-Parents:</u> Apply these questions to a sibling, niece/nephew, or children of a close friend.

Date Answered

Q136

I am struggling to love (name). Open my eyes to see (name) as You do. How do I love (name) in a way he/she can receive it?

Date Answered

Q137

How would a mentor/coach help me at this time? Where do I find one?

Date Answered

Q138

Is there an area that I have compromised Your best for me? How can I change to get back on track?

_____
Date Answered

Q139

What do You wish I wanted to change about me that I have been resistant or ignorant of?

_____
Date Answered

Q140

Show me what a godly, married couple looks like. What makes them so different?

_____
Date Answered

Q141

Do I have an emotional closet that I have locked and kept from You? How do I unlock it and let You in?

_____
Date Answered

Q142

How can I live more in the present versus the past or the future? I want to enjoy each moment You give me, so how do I stay focused on the here and now so I can connect with You easily?

_____
Date Answered

Q143

Is there an area of my life that I am not trusting You with – an area that I am striving in or trying to control?

_____
Date Answered

Q144

Is there an area of my heart that needs healing? How would You like to heal it?

_____
Date Answered

Q145

What area of communication skills do I need to work on and how do I do that?

_____
Date Answered

Q146

How do I view authority? How should I view authority? How can I love those who are in authority over me?

Date Answered

Q147

What have I not shown You gratitude for?

Date Answered

Q148

Is there anything in my life stealing my heart away from You that I have made into an idol?

Date Answered

Q149

What is an area of my life that I thought it was too hard for You to deal with or change?

Date Answered

Q150

If I could have freedom in one area of my life, what area do You want it to be? How do I partner with You to walk in that freedom?

_____
Date Answered

Q151

What are the wrong beliefs You want to show me? Where is my thinking off track with Yours? What is the truth You want me to replace these thoughts with?

_____
Date Answered

Q152

If married: God, tell me how You see my spouse. What do You want to say to me about my marriage? How do You want me to see my marriage?
If single: What qualities do I need to develop in order to be a good match for someone else?

_____
Date Answered

Q153

Where in my life, have I become too comfortable? What needs to change?

_____
Date Answered

Q154

<u>If married:</u> What would You have me do to enhance the feeling of honor, respect, and love that my spouse needs from me right now?
<u>If single:</u> What would You have me do to enhance the feeling of honor, respect and love that my family needs from me right now?

_____
Date Answered

Q155

God, I don't feel like I am getting answers about (<u>situation/problem</u>). Holy Spirit, do You have a better question for me to ask?

_____
Date Answered

Q156

Jesus, is there someone who was instrumental or prayed for me to come to know You?
How can I thank them?

_____
Date Answered

Q157

<u>Parents:</u> What special needs do each of my children have that You, God, want me to meet? Are there weaknesses You want me to pray about and come along side to strengthen?
<u>Non-Parents:</u> Apply these questions to a sibling, niece/nephew, or children of a close friend.

_____
Date Answered

Q158

What will people say about me at my funeral? If that is different than how I want to be remembered, how can I change my life to make it more like how I want to be remembered?

_____
Date Answered

Q159

How can I become refreshed when I feel empty?

_____
Date Answered

Q160

<u>Parents:</u> How can I nurture my relationship with each of my children?
<u>Non-Parents:</u> Whose child do I nurture a relationship with so that I encourage and build up their family?

_____
Date Answered

Q161

What is in my life that You consider unhealthy or toxic?

_____
Date Answered

Q162

What healing do I need in order to enter into this next season without baggage that would hinder my progress?

_____
Date Answered

Q163

What relationships do I need to prioritize in my life now and what does it look like?

_____
Date Answered

Q164

What changes do I need to make to be
healthier for this next season?

_____
Date Answered

Q165

What personal prisons have I built out of fears?
What is my biggest fear and how
can we deal with it?

_____
Date Answered

Q166

How have I sabotaged myself in the past few years?
What do I need to do to keep from sabotaging
myself in the future?

_____
Date Answered

Q167

Is there someplace in my life that I am "stuck"?
How do I partner with You to get unstuck?

_____
Date Answered

Q168

Lord, am I expressing myself authentically, or have my interactions been artificial and contrived?

_____
Date Answered

Q169

God, I love you! What blocks me from moving forward in my relationship with You? How can these blockages best be dealt with?

_____
Date Answered

Q170

Everyone has had some sort of trauma in their lives. Where is trauma in my life and how would You like to remove it and heal me?

_____
Date Answered

Q171

Are there relationships in my past that I am still "tied" to in some ungodly way? I choose to cut the ungodly ties with these people by praying this prayer: *"In the name of Jesus, I cut and loose all ungodly ties and attachments with (name) and I loose myself from any and all ungodly attachments and ties with (name). In the name of Jesus, I bless (name)."* Record your experience.

_____
Date Answered

Q172

Visualize handing all of your worries, schedule, to do lists, etc. to Jesus. Then tell God that you choose to enter into His rest. Visualize walking into His rest like it is a cloud in front of you.
Record your experience.

_____
Date Answered

Q173

Bring each member of your immediate family to God in prayer and ask Him how to pray for each one and what His heart is for them. Come into agreement with God in prayer.

_____
Date Answered

Q174

Read *1 Corinthians 13:4-7* as if you are speaking about yourself. Now Ask God: Is this how You see me? What do I need to work on in order to love better? How do I do that?

_____
Date Answered

Q175

Do I have any walls that keep You at a distance? What are they and how can we bring them down so that there is no hindrance to my relationship with You?

_____
Date Answered

Q176

What have I failed at recently? God, how do You
view this failure? How could I
do things differently next time?

_____
Date Answered

Q177

God, how can my relationship with You be
strengthened as a result of the struggle I am going
through right now? How do I "count it all joy"?
(Romans 5:3-5; James 1:2-4)

_____
Date Answered

Q178

What is my biggest struggle in life right now from
Your perspective? What provision and/or promise is
attached to this struggle that I am going through?

_____
Date Answered

Q179

Holy Spirit, are there areas that I need to forgive my
birth mother for? How would You like me to forgive
her and enter into healing and wholeness?

_____
Date Answered

Q180

How do I partner with You, Holy Spirit,
to allow breakthrough to occur?

Date Answered

Q181

What act of kindness can I do today?

Date Answered

Q182

What is something in my life that I've seen as a loss
that actually made room in my life for more of You?

Date Answered

Q183

Holy Spirit, I am grieving and mourning over
(person/situation). Help me experience who You are
as my Comforter in this. How do You want me to
pray for this (person/situation)?

Date Answered

Q184

Jesus, what would You say today to my
inner critic – the voice that is always telling
me "I am not good enough"?

Date Answered

Q185

Father God, are there areas that I need to forgive
my birth father for? How would you like me to
forgive him and enter into healing and wholeness?

Date Answered

Q186

<u>Parents:</u> Is there anything You want me to do to
help nurture my children's walk with You?
<u>Non-Parents:</u> How can I nurture the relationship
with You in the children that I have connection with?

Date Answered

Q187

Jesus, where in my life do I keep telling myself
I am unclean, but You say I am clean already?

Date Answered

Q188
Holy Spirit, how do You see greatness in how I am navigating my current challenges?

_____
Date Answered

Q189
Father God, when I look back at some of the difficulties I've encountered, I often remember my failures and lack. What is Your point of view on what I've been through?

_____
Date Answered

Q190
Jesus, an area I feel ashamed about is _____. It is hard to come to You while I feel so unworthy, but here I am. How do You want to touch me right now?

_____
Date Answered

Q191
Father God, what are You delighted to set free within me today?

_____
Date Answered

Q192

Where in my life do You want to say, "It's Me, God, don't be afraid!"?

Date Answered

Q193

What brings Your peace to me?
How do I tap into Your peace?

Date Answered

Q194

In order for me to enter into my next season, what habits need to change?

Date Answered

Q195

Am I stewarding authority and influence well? Where am I doing well and where do I need to grow in? How do I grow in this?

Date Answered

Q196

In what area of my life am I feeling hopeless? What do I need to believe to have hope?

Date Answered

Q197

What is one thing I'm doing/believing right now that makes You sad? Why? What is one thing I'm doing/believing right now that makes You glad? Why?

_____
Date Answered

Q198

Is there a part of me that is shut-down or weary that You want to awaken and heal?

_____
Date Answered

Q199

What do I need to unlearn? What new mindsets should I be viewing my situations through?

_____
Date Answered

Q200

How big is my faith right now?
How can I increase it?

_____
Date Answered

Q201

When have I been too hard on myself?
What do You say about those times?

_____
Date Answered

Q202
Is there some way that I am not honoring my body as the temple of God? What needs to change?
(*1 Corinthians 3:16-17*)

_____
Date Answered

Q203
As a minister of reconciliation, how can I bring reconciliation into my family, church, friendships, etc.? (*2 Corinthians 5:18-19*)

_____
Date Answered

Q204
How should I view other people's opinions of me?

_____
Date Answered

Q205
Is there an area of my life that I am insecure? How do I enter into Your security in that area?

_____
Date Answered

Q206
Where do I seek comfort when I am hurting? Where should I seek comfort?

_____
Date Answered

Q207

God, I would like some advice/wisdom about (situation/problem). What do you have to say about it?

_____
Date Answered

Q208

How do I view discipline? How should I view it?

_____
Date Answered

Q209

Is my heart open to loving others and being loved? What keeps me from fully loving and being loved?

_____
Date Answered

Q210

There have been some very difficult/painful times in my life, like (situation). How would You like to redeem this for my good? *(Romans 8:28)* How can I partner with You for freedom and healing from this difficult situation?

_____
Date Answered

Q211

Are there areas of my life that I am more of a victim than a victor? What is the truth?

_____
Date Answered

Q212

Are there any careless words I have spoken or others have spoken over my life that are actually curses? Examples: "You can't do anything right!" "I am always getting sick." "I never have enough money."
Pray to renounce those curses:
"Father, in the name of Jesus, I repent, renounce, and break all agreement with all word curses that were spoken to me, by me, or over me. I renounce and break the curses of (name or describe them) in Jesus' name. I give and receive the blessings of God in their place. In Jesus' name. Amen.
Record your experience.

_____
Date Answered

Q213

Jesus, You are not confined by time or space. You are always with me. Do I have a memory that You want to heal? Would you take me back to that memory to bring healing and freedom by encountering me there?

_____
Date Answered

Q214

God, would you show me how unforgiveness is keeping me from moving on with You? Who do I need to forgive? (parents, siblings, friends, work associates, teachers, etc.)

_____
Date Answered

Q215

Is there someone I have hurt and need to ask them to forgive me? How do you want me to do it?

_____
Date Answered

Q216

Is there anything in my home that is hurting me or causing me to stumble? How do you want me to deal with it?

_____
Date Answered

Q217

Where am I prideful? What triggers my pride? How can I walk in true humility?

_____
Date Answered

Q218

Who do I have around me that could be
encouraging insecurity, doubt or self-consciousness
in me? How can I build confidence Your way instead
of the world's way?

_____
Date Answered

Q219

How can my heart have enough capacity to love
people who have hurt me or the ones I love?

_____
Date Answered

Q220

Lust perverts things. I don't want to walk in lust
and perversion. Are there things in my life that are
opening that door to me? Are there people around
me that are enabling this in my life?

_____
Date Answered

Q221

Holy Spirit, are there some limiting beliefs (lies)
from my parents that I am walking in? Can I give
them to You? What would You like to give me in
exchange for them that will shift me into a
new paradigm of thinking?

_____
Date Answered

Q222

Father God, how do I view failure?
Do I avoid it at all costs? If so, why?

_____
Date Answered

Q223

Lord, please show me three people I need to make myself more available to. What should I do today and this week to connect with them?

_____
Date Answered

Q224

God, am I a procrastinator? If so, how can I change so that I do what I need to do when I need to do it?

_____
Date Answered

Q225

What would it look like to be 100% free from caring what other people think about me?
How do I get there?

_____
Date Answered

Q226

Holy Spirit, are there some Bible verses that I need to meditate on when I am feeling down?
What are they?

Date Answered

Q227

Jesus, show me how You stand next to me as my Saving Hero to rescue me from all my accusers.
"For you stand right next to the broken ones as their saving hero to rescue them from all their accusers."
(Psalm 109:31 - TPT)

Date Answered

Q228

How am I forgiven, Jesus?
Help me understand Your forgiveness more deeply.

Date Answered

Q229

God, are You safe? Will you hurt me if I surrender fully to You?

Date Answered

Q230

Father God, on a scale of 1 to 10 – with one being "very little" and ten being "all the time" – how much does ungodly fear have a hold of my life?

_____
Date Answered

Q231

How are You and I doing in our relationship?

_____
Date Answered

Q232

God, how can my relationship with You improve? Are there disciplines I need to put in place? What are they?

_____
Date Answered

Q233

Would You remind me of the blessings You poured out on me in the past few days?

_____
Date Answered

Q234

How happy would I be if I had zero attachment to material things?

_____
Date Answered

Q235

What is one thing in my life that You are telling me to let go of? Why don't I need it?

_____
Date Answered

Q236

What is one thing not in my life that You are telling me to put into my life? Why do I need it?

_____
Date Answered

Q237

What does entering into the "joy of the Lord" look like for me today?
(Isaiah 29:19; Matthew 25:21,23)

_____
Date Answered

Q238

Is there someone I need to show gratitude to for their impact on my life? How should I go about that?

_____
Date Answered

Q239

Is there someone I need to be praying for right now? How do I need to be praying for them? Do I let them know I was praying for them?

_____
Date Answered

Q240

Jesus, with everything there is to do, it's hard to stay in the easy yoke with You. *(Matthew 11:28-30)* What do You want to say about all the things on my to do list today?

_____
Date Answered

Q241

You are the potter and I am the clay. *(Isaiah 64:8)* Would You give me a picture of what my clay looks like now and what I will look like when You are done?

_____
Date Answered

Q242

Bring one of your nighttime dreams to Jesus to ask for His interpretation of it. Write down the dream and interpretation. Run it past some other believers who understand dreams.

_____
Date Answered

WHOLENESS DISCOVERY / 81

Q243
Do You have a gift for me today? What is it? Why do I need it? What do I do with it?

_____
Date Answered

Q244
Papa God, how old am I in the Spirit? How do I enjoy this age and learn what I need to learn? What can I do to mature and grow?

_____
Date Answered

Q245
Jesus, I'm feeling bad because I haven't spent much time with You in the last couple days. What do You want to say to me about that?

_____
Date Answered

Q246
How do You view my past mistakes and sins?

_____
Date Answered

Q247

Holy Spirit, I over reacted (anger, tears, frustration…) to a situation that should not have had that kind of reaction. There must be a wound or something I am believing that caused that reaction. What is it and how do I deal with it?

_____
Date Answered

Q248

I can see patterns of behavior in my family line that is hurting me and others. How do I break free of this generational behavior?

_____
Date Answered

Q249

Sometimes I shut down and stop communicating. What is inside of me that keeps me from sharing and connecting? How do I deal with it?

_____
Date Answered

Q250

How will my walking in more wholeness and healing affect my family and friends?

_____
Date Answered

SELF DISCOVERY

WHO AM I?
WHAT IS MY CALLING/DESTINY?

"For I know the thoughts that I think toward you,"
says the Lord, "thoughts of peace and not of evil,
to give you a future and a hope."
(Jeremiah 29:11)

Q251

What is my #1 strength?
What are my other strengths?

_____
Date Answered

Q252

*"Before I formed you in the womb,
I knew you." (Jeremiah 1:5)*
What were you thinking when You dreamed of me?

_____
Date Answered

Q253

Is there a people group, community, city, state or country that you are calling me to? How do you want me to pray into this area?

_____
Date Answered

Q254

What would You like to see me accomplish in the next 6 months?

_____
Date Answered

Q255

What is the dream that You have put
into my heart to do?

Date Answered

Q256

What positive legacy has my mom
passed down to me?

Date Answered

Q257

What positive legacy has my dad
passed down to me?

Date Answered

Q258

What would be a good "warning label" for me?
(For example: Requires adventure in order to
function at peak level.
Needs affirmation periodically.)

Date Answered

Q259

What are the gifts, talents, and abilities
that You have given me?

_____
Date Answered

Q260

Jesus, what do You love about me?
What quality do You love the most about me?

_____
Date Answered

Q261

Out of 7 billion people on the planet, what makes
me unique or different from everyone else?

_____
Date Answered

Q262

What goals have I set and reached during the
past 5 years? What goals have I set and failed to
achieve during that period? What kept me from
meeting my goals?

_____
Date Answered

Q263

What dream did I lay down that I need
to pick up again?

_____
Date Answered

Q264

If I were able to tap into my full potential
for 1 year, what could I do?

_____
Date Answered

Q265

What does evangelism look like when it is flowing
through me with my gifts, talents and abilities?

_____
Date Answered

Q266

Is there a gift/talent in me that I have not
developed or tapped into fully?

_____
Date Answered

Q267

Is there one person I need to be praying for
regarding their salvation?
How do You want me to pray for him/her?

_____
Date Answered

Q268

Lord, I want to make a list of what I really want in life. Would you help me and remind me of what I am passionate about?

_____
Date Answered

Q269

What's the biggest risk You want me to take and what will be the outcome?

_____
Date Answered

Q270

Is there somebody who is doing what I want to do that I can have as a mentor to me?

_____
Date Answered

Q271

All of us tend to have things we are passionate about that we are called to. Are there some passions I have not recognized as callings?

_____
Date Answered

Q272

What drives me? What is my core need?
What am I willing to sacrifice or take risks for?

_____
Date Answered

Q273

What is my greatest challenge in life right now?

_____
Date Answered

Q274

Lord, what is the primary ministry You would have me doing at this time? How can I be more effective in this ministry?

_____
Date Answered

Q275

What skills or knowledge do I need to pursue my dreams? How could I improve my skill and expertise in these areas?

_____
Date Answered

Q276

Lord, as You look at my dreams, what are Your thoughts? How do You see them?

_____
Date Answered

Q277

Is there something unfinished from this year or the year before that I need to finish?

_____
Date Answered

Q278

What are You calling me to in this next season? Is there something you want me to start in this next season?

_____
Date Answered

Q279

Are there any major things in the next season that I need to know about or prepare for? What do I need to learn for this next season? Are there books to read? Is there research I need to do?

_____
Date Answered

Q280

Who will I need to be now, that I have never been before?

_____
Date Answered

Q280

What will I need to do in this season
that I've never done before?

Date Answered

Q282

*"We have become His poetry, a re-created people
that will fulfill the destiny He has given each of us,
for we are joined to Jesus, the Anointed One. Even
before we were born, God planned in advance our
destiny and the good works we would do to fulfill it."
(Ephesians 2:10 - TPT)*

What are the good works You have created for me?

Date Answered

Q283

Is there a secret You can tell me about my destiny
and calling? Can I share it with others or
is it just for You and me?

Date Answered

Q284

Are there a few words/Scriptures I am to focus on
for this year? What Words/Promises/Scriptures
should I stand on for victory and/or my future?

Date Answered

Q285

What can I change in my life to hear Your voice more clearly?

_____
Date Answered

Q286

The Israelites followed your cloud by day and fire by night. Am I still following You or have I stayed in a place that you are no longer leading me in?

_____
Date Answered

Q287

God, why did You give me the name I have? What does it say about me and my purpose?

_____
Date Answered

Q288

What would I do different if no one would judge me? How do I walk in freedom from fear of man?

_____
Date Answered

Q289

Am I using my gifts to serve and elevate others?
How can I use my gifts to impact
others in a positive way?

_____
Date Answered

Q290

Are there routines in my life that have too strong a
grip on my life, and are keeping me from advancing
on to my newer, more beautiful ambitions?

_____
Date Answered

Q291

God, what promises in Your Word are for me now?

_____
Date Answered

Q292

Would You show me what the enemy does
not want me to see? What do I need
to do with this information?

_____
Date Answered

Q293

What will my life look like one year from now, three years from now, five years from now,
ten years from now…?

———————————
Date Answered

Q294

On a scale of 1 to 10 with 1 feeling more like a servant/slave and 10 feeling more like Your son/daughter, where am I? How did I get here?

———————————
Date Answered

Q295

How can I move closer to my true identity
as Your son/daughter?

———————————
Date Answered

Q296

When You look at me, what do You see? How can I see the image of me that You see? What beautiful part of me did You create that I have yet to see?

———————————
Date Answered

SELF DISCOVERY / 95

Q297

I am seated with You in Heavenly places.
(Philippians 3:20; Ephesians 2:6)
Since I am seated with You, I can hear Your voice.
What can I see/hear from this position
that I can't otherwise?

Date Answered

Q298

How have I moved out of humble trust in You and tried to rush Your purposes in my life? When have I worked in the flesh to try and accomplish what only You can do?
(Repent for those activities and surrender to the Holy Spirit's working and timing in your life.)

Date Answered

Q299

Your Word (Scripture and Revelation) is many things. *(Psalm 119:105; John 17:17; Romans 10:17; 2 Timothy 3:16)* Lord, reveal how I am to wield the "sword of the Spirit which is the Word of God". *(Ephesians 6:17)*

Date Answered

Q300

What do I already have that I may have overlooked
or did not consider for this next season?

_____
Date Answered

Q301

If the thoughts I have been thinking recently
ultimately become my destiny, am I on the right
path? What thoughts do I need to change in order
to align with Your dreams for my life?
What thoughts should I have?

_____
Date Answered

Q302

Papa God, what quality do You see in me
that most reminds You of Jesus?

_____
Date Answered

Q303

What is one way that I am created in Your image
that I haven't realized yet?

_____
Date Answered

Q304

Jesus, _____ is something I deeply desire that I haven't even had the courage to ask You for. How do you feel about this?

_____
Date Answered

Q305

Would You give me a picture just for me, so that I can understand how valuable I am to You.

_____
Date Answered

Q306

Jesus, where do You see courage in me?

_____
Date Answered

Q307

Jesus, I often feel like I'm sitting in the boat, watching others take leaps of faith that I'm too scared to attempt. I feel like I'm such a slow learner in this. How do You feel about my progress?

_____
Date Answered

Q308

Father, sometimes I'm embarrassed to keep asking You for _____. How do you feel about it when I don't give up and I keep bringing this to You?

_____
Date Answered

Q309

What do you love about how I've invested my life in following You?

_____
Date Answered

Q310

How have You confirmed the dreams in my heart?

_____
Date Answered

Q311

What resources do I need to do what You have called me to? Where and how do I get them?

_____
Date Answered

Q312

Have I been double-minded in regards to how I think about myself and my destiny? Thinking one way but acting another? What areas need to come into a singular focus?

_____
Date Answered

Q313

What are you doing in me in this season?

_____
Date Answered

Q314

What keeps showing up in my life that illustrates to me some of my destiny?

_____
Date Answered

Q315

What am I more passionate about: doing, leading, loving or learning? Why?

_____
Date Answered

Q316

What specific areas of my life do I need to begin speaking success and hope over right now? What is Your truth about these areas?

_____
Date Answered

Q317

What part do I play in building Your Kingdom through my church?

_____
Date Answered

Q318

What goals am I afraid to set because I feel incapable of reaching them? If You could write out 3 goals for the season I am in, what would they be?

_____
Date Answered

Q319

What does victory look like for me this year?

_____
Date Answered

Q320

Father God, what were my biggest accomplishments this past year?

_____
Date Answered

Q321

Father God, is my current daily routine structured to optimize time for Your priorities?
How should it change?

Date Answered

Q322

When and how will I see the fruits of this season in my life?

Date Answered

Q323

Father God, do You think I'm beautiful/handsome?
Why do You think that?

Date Answered

Q324

Is there anything that I need to put on my bucket list that isn't there now?

Date Answered

Q325

Sometimes, I feel like I wear a mask around people.
Who am I under the mask?

Date Answered

Q326

Have I messed up so badly that I have missed out on Your best for me? What is Your best?

_____
Date Answered

Q327

What is my value based on?
Does what I have to say have value?

_____
Date Answered

Q328

Do I measure up in Your eyes?
Do I have unrealistic expectations of myself?

_____
Date Answered

Q329

Why did you create me to be a man/woman?
Why was I born to my family and have the brothers and sisters I have?

_____
Date Answered

Q330

Do I live more by the love of the law or by the law of love?

_____
Date Answered

Q331

Sometimes, I strive for the approval and acceptance of man more than resting in my position of being totally accepted in Your love and justified by grace. How can I stay in that place of not caring about man's opinion of me and living in Your total acceptance?

_____
Date Answered

Q332

Are the motivations of my heart pure when I do service/ministry for the Kingdom? Do they need to change? How?

_____
Date Answered

Q333

On a scale of 1 to 10 with 1 having the heart of an orphan and 10 having the heart of Your son/daughter, where am I? How can I move closer to thinking like Your son/daughter?

_____
Date Answered

Q334

Father God, how have You revealed my true identity to me?

_____
Date Answered

Q335

As I look over my life, what have You been
saying to me throughout my life?

Date Answered

Q336

Where is my mission field?
How do you want me to share You in this place?

Date Answered

Q337

What if I did something different for my future?
What could I do?

Date Answered

Q338

Lord, I see this (need) in my community.
What can I offer to meet that need?

Date Answered

Q339

Why is it harmful to the Body of Christ when I don't
know who I am and walk in my true identity?

Date Answered

Q340

Holy Spirit, have I given my talents and gifts too much weight regarding my sense of identity and self-worth? Am I seeing myself as more of a "human doing" versus a "human being"?

_____
Date Answered

Q341

What kind of fruit am I producing right now?

_____
Date Answered

Q342

Jesus, is there something in my life that I should stop doing so that I can make room for something You want me to do or I really want to do?

_____
Date Answered

Q343

What have You spoken over my life and destiny? Does my heart believe what You have said? How can my heart come into agreement with You? How can I speak and declare success based on those revelations?

_____
Date Answered

Q344

What kind of strategies do I need now to prevent the enemy from stealing, killing and destroying me and my destiny? (*John 10:10*)

_____
Date Answered

Q345

What can I learn about myself from those who oppose me and seek to hinder my destiny? ("Those" may refer to the devil or the devil working through people)

_____
Date Answered

Q346

Am I guarding my eyes and ears? If not, what am I letting into my heart that doesn't belong there? Do I need to stop watching or listening to some things? What are they?

_____
Date Answered

Q347

Even though I may not want to share my dream with certain people, I do want to be able to articulate it clearly - even if I only say it to myself. Show me how to write down my dream in 1-2 sentences. Who are the cheerleaders in my life that I can share my dream with and know they will wholeheartedly support me?

_____
Date Answered

Q348

How is my relationship with You, God? Am I enjoying Your presencein intimate worship? If not, what can I do to put myself in a position to do so?

_____
Date Answered

Q349

What problem in the world did You create me to solve? What does Your solution, through me, look like? How can I partner with You to solve this problem?

_____
Date Answered

Q350

Sometimes I feel like a round peg trying to fit into a square hole. What am I striving to fit into that you didn't call me to? Where do I fit?

_____
Date Answered

Q351

In *Revelation 2:17*, You say that you will *"give him a white stone, and on the stone a new name written which no one knows except him who receives it."* Can I know what that new name is for me? What does this name mean for my identity in You?

_____
Date Answered

Q352

Lord, what is the next thing I should work on that is on my bucket list? What is my first step?

_____
Date Answered

Q353

Father God, what rights and privileges do I have as Your son/daughter? What does that give me and how should I see it?

_____
Date Answered

Q354

What if the churches in my community came together to advance Your Kingdom? What could we accomplish?

_____
Date Answered

Q355

Is there a Bible verse(s) that I should memorize and meditate on? Why did You choose that verse(s) for me?

———————————
Date Answered

Q356

What season of life am I in?

———————————
Date Answered

Q357

What is something adventurous that You would like to see me do?

———————————
Date Answered

Q358

If I were a Christian rapper, what would You want my rapper name to be?

———————————
Date Answered

Q359

Is there some symbolic act I should do to step into what You have for me? For example, "opening a door" or "jumping into another room".

———————————
Date Answered

Q360

What Bible character best describes
my destiny and why?

_____
Date Answered

Q361

Jesus, what spiritual weapon do I need for this next
season? What is it used for? Receive the
weapon from the Lord.

_____
Date Answered

Q362

Is there someone who would do great damage
to the enemy's kingdom if he/she came to know
Jesus? How can I pray for them?

_____
Date Answered

Q363

Ask God to bring someone to your mind that needs
encouragement. Write a letter of encouragement for
them and include Scriptures God gives you.
Give or mail it to them.

_____
Date Answered

SELF DISCOVERY

Q364

Father God, what is something I can
use my faith on today?

_____
Date Answered

Q365

Jesus, what's one thing that looks like an
impossible challenge to me that You say we
can tackle together?

_____
Date Answered

Q366

Tell me something about my neighbors that You
love. How can I better show them Your love?

_____
Date Answered

Q367

How is the favor of God working in my life for my
benefit right now?

_____
Date Answered

Q368

Is there something that I can do
to increase my income?

_____
Date Answered

Q369

Do You have some type of invention or idea that You want to give me to create?

_____
Date Answered

Q370

What does revival look like?
How can I partner with You to bring it into my area?

_____
Date Answered

Q371

If you made a movie of my life, what would You want it named?

_____
Date Answered

Q372

How do You view money and getting rich?
Lord, what's Your definition of success?

_____
Date Answered

Q373

There are so many aspects of Your character. Who will You be for me now that You have never been before?

_____
Date Answered

Q374

What is one thing You are doing in my city?
What is one thing You are doing in my nation?
How can I come into agreement with You in action and prayer?

_____
Date Answered

Q375

Develop declarations of what God has spoken over you regarding who you are and
what you are called to do.

_____
Date Answered

Appendix

SYMBOL MEANINGS -- NUMBERS

1 = GOD, first, new, unity, quality of God, unique value of individual

2 = multiplication, divide, judge, separate, discern, powers, persons, completeness, testimony

3 = Godhead (TRIUNE GOD), thoroughness, finality, totality, significance

4 = reign, rule, kingdom, God's creative works, completeness, salvation or judgment, worldwide spread of God's kingdom over the earth

5 = grace, redemption, anointing, recompense, bounteous reward

6 = man, carnal, humanity, world given over to judgment, broken world kingdom

7 = completion, perfection, fullness, rest, fullness of divine identity, release from toil

8 = new beginnings (resulting from putting off the old), new era and life - TEACHER

9 = Judgment – EVANGELIST – works of Holy Spirit

10 = journey, wilderness, nurture, perfected universality - PASTOR

11 = transition, standing in the gap - PROPHET

12 = government, restoration, God fulfills promises of redemption, church - APOSTLE

13 = rebellion

14 = double anointing

15 = reprieve, mercy

16 = established new beginnings

17 = elect of God

25 = begin ministry training

30 = begin ministry

37 = First born, prime number (3X37=111)

40 = generational and completed rule, hardship, affliction, punishment, wilderness, probation, chastisement, humiliation

50 = jubilee, maturity, respect, completion, wisdom of long experience, liberty, freedom
70 = mark of leadership, military strength, judgment
77 = unrestricted and unsurpassable fullness
100 = completeness, complete blessing
111 = My Beloved Son
120 = end of flesh
153 = kingdom multiplication
666 = full lawlessness
888 = resurrection
1000 = large quantity, relatively large number
1500 = light, power, authority

COLORS

Rainbow:	covenant promises, God keeps promises
Gold/ Amber:	(+) holy, purity, glory (-) idolatry, defilement, licentiousness (lawless/immoral)
Blue:	(+) communion, revelation (-) depression, sorrow, anxiety
Silver:	(+) redemption (-) legalism, slavery, domination
Red:	(+) wisdom, anointing, power, blood of sacrifice to bring cleansing (-) anger, war
Purple:	(+) authority, royalty, power, wealth (-) false authority, licentiousness (lawless/immoral)
Green:	(+) conscience, growth, prosperity (-) envy, jealousy, pride
Magenta:	(+) emotions, love (-) hate
White:	(+) Spirit of the Lord, holy power, purity, transition from guilt to purity, God's forgiveness, redemption, absence of darkness (-) religious spirit
Brown:	(+) compassion, humility (-) humanism
Yellow:	(+) mind, hope, gift of God (-) fear, coward, intellectual pride
Cyan:	(+) will, perseverance (-) strong willed

Orange: (+) perseverance
(-) stubbornness, strong willed
Black: (-) God's judgment, darkness

ABOUT THE AUTHOR

Gloria Gierach has been pursuing God since she was 14 years old. She has held many hats over her 65+ years but none are as precious to her as a "beloved daughter of the King". There are accolades that could be shared for her "credentials" but none of them seem to matter to her. She likes to describe herself as "A disciple of Jesus Christ skillfully disguised as a dull homemaker".

Gloria has been married to her beloved, Rich, for 44 years and is the mother to 7 adult children and their spouses and grandmother to 13 grandchildren. She homeschooled her children for 26 years. They live in Hartland, Wisconsin.

Gloria and Rich started a ministry in 2008 called 3:20 Ministries -- a ministry called to inspire, lead and equip people to live a Christ-centered, abundant lifestyle of freedom. They release people to fulfill God's purpose and destiny through life-changing God encounters that facilitate authentic healing. 3:20 stands for *Ephesians 3:20 "Now to him who is able to do immeasurably more than all we ask or imagine, according to his power that is at work within us."*

Gloria teaches "Hearing God Workshops" and "Setting Your Church Free" events. She also enjoys speaking at conferences and retreats. She loves to teach people how to hear and encounter God for themselves.

Other resources Gloria has developed include:

"Conversation Starters with God Journal" is the same as this book but with space to journal the answers to the questions.

"Conversation Starters for Christians" is a game with questions specifically designed to create connection, community and faith.

"Forgiving Parents" Study for individuals and small groups. A video and study package to walk people through the sometimes difficult task of forgiving their parents.

Coming soon: "The Rock Files" – Lessons learned from life.

All of these resources can be found at:
https://CrossFireExchange.com

Made in the USA
Monee, IL
07 March 2023